FIFTY ART SONGS

by Nineteenth-Century Masters

Edited by Henry T. Finck

For High Voice

Dover Publications, Inc., New York

Published in Canada by General Publishing Company, Ltd., 30 Lesmill Road, Don Mills, Toronto, Ontario.

Published in the United Kingdom by Constable and Company, Ltd., 10 Orange Street, London WC 2.

This Dover edition, first published in 1975, is an unabridged republication of the work originally published under the title *Fifty Mastersongs* by the Oliver Ditson Company, Boston, in 1903 in the series "The Musicians Library." The present edition is published by special arrangement with the Theodore Presser Company, Bryn Mawr, Pennsylvania.

International Standard Book Number: 0-486-23193-3
Library of Congress Catalog Card Number: 75-12131

Manufactured in the United States of America
Dover Publications, Inc.
180 Varick Street
New York, N.Y. 10014

CONTENTS

LISZT   TCHAÏKOVSKY   RUBINSTEIN

SCHUMANN   SCHUBERT   FRANZ

GRIEG   BRAHMS   JENSEN

INDEX OF AUTHORS

INDEX OF AUTHORS

FIFTY MASTERSONGS

A FEW years ago it was the fashion to print lists of the best hundred books. Naturally, no two of these lists were alike, for men differ widely in taste and judgment. The same result would follow if a number of experts and amateurs were asked to make a list of the best hundred songs—or let us say fifty—which is as many as can be conveniently printed in one volume.

The editor of the present collection of Fifty Mastersongs has made a special study of this branch of music for more than a quarter of a century; and while writing his recent volume, *Songs and Song Writers*, he had to go over the whole ground once more carefully. He therefore realizes vividly the difficulty of making the wisest possible choice. The chief perplexity arises from the superabundance of good things. Among Schubert's songs alone, for instance, there are more than fifty which clamor for admission; but only a few can be inserted, because room must be left for other masters.

The aim has been to secure as much variety as possible without falling below a certain standard. For this reason Mozart, Beethoven, and a few other composers are represented, even though none of their songs quite equal the best by Schubert, Schumann, Franz, or Grieg.

While, for the reasons given, it cannot be claimed that the songs in this volume are absolutely the best fifty ever written, it may be confidently asserted that they are fifty of the best. They are all mastersongs, bearing the hall-mark of genius and originality, and each one is characteristic of its composer. Familiarity with them will breed more and more admiration; and if you come across one that you do not like at first, you may be sure that the fault is yours: either you do not interpret it correctly, or your pianist is a bungler, or you need to hear it half a dozen times before you can fathom its charms; for the beauty of these songs is more than skin-deep.

Fashionable songs please only for a few weeks, while mastersongs are among the things of beauty which are a joy forever. It is sad to think how much time and money are wasted on trashy music. Singers go into music-stores and buy pebbles and glass beads when for the same money, or even less, they might get genuine diamonds and pearls. One of the objects in issuing this collection is to so train the taste of amateurs that they will be able henceforth to tell real diamonds and pearls from their worthless imitations.

Some surprise may be caused by the fact that there are no Italian and only two French songs in this collection. The editor has searched far and wide for an Italian song worthy of being included, but without success, for reasons which cannot be given here, but which may be found in *Songs and Song Writers*, pp. 218-227. Liszt has remarked justly that the lyric art-song, or *Lied*, is "poetically and musically a product peculiar to the Germanic muse." Nevertheless, of our fifty mastersongs only twenty-nine are by German composers—Mozart, Beethoven, Schubert, Schumann, Wagner, Franz, Cornelius, Brahms, Jensen, Strauss. The Norwegian Grieg contributes six; the Russian Rubinstein and Tchaïkovsky five; the Hungarian Liszt three; the Polish Chopin and Paderewski three; the French Massenet and Godard two; the Bohemian Dvořák and the American MacDowell one each. So that from the national point of view, too, we have considerable variety. America, it may be added, would have been represented more liberally had it not been for copyright difficulties.

Special attention has been given in this volume to the translations. Most translators sacrifice sense, accent, and everything else to the foolish effort at securing rhymes. Wherever this had been done in the case of songs here used, new versions have been specially made for this collection, in pursuance of the publisher's determination to make this volume first-class in every detail.

HINTS TO SINGERS

REMEMBER that the public likes good music as well as good singing, and that those vocalists are most likely to succeed in the long run who combine the two. What is wanted to-day is not simply songs but mastersongs.

A singer may have ever so beautiful a voice, and phrase with ever so much taste; if he does not enunciate the words distinctly, he is no better than a flute-player or a violinist. Most singers produce nothing but what has been aptly called "inarticulate smudges of sound," comparable to the illegible figures on a worn coin.

Technique is important, but expression is even more so. The one thing which to-day has artistic and financial value in the musical world is temperament—the power to stir an audience with emotion. To do so, the singer must enter into the spirit of the poem, just as if he were going to speak it on the stage without music.

The pianist should neither drown the voice nor act as if he were a mere accompanist; for his part is usually quite as important as the singer's. He should study the text as carefully as the vocalist does; because in the songs the piano part is often descriptive and highly emotional, and the player is at sea unless he knows what the poem is about.

Careful attention to the poetic text also makes it easier to get the right tempo—a matter of vital importance, as a trifle too fast or too slow may utterly mar a song. Nor is it enough to have the general pace right. There are constant modifications of tempo, and of loudness, and special accents, which are the very life of the music. Take, for instance, that superbly emotional song, Grieg's *The Swan*. Unless both singer and player heed the expression marks—*andante ben tenuto, poco animato, crescendo, agitato, ritenuto, tranquillo, lento*—the song becomes like a rose without perfume, like a bird of paradise without feathers.

WOLFGANG AMADEUS MOZART (1756–1791)
AND
LUDWIG VAN BEETHOVEN (1770–1827)

WHILE simple folk-songs have always existed, the lyric art-song, in which the pianoforte part is as important as the vocal melody, is practically a product of the nineteenth century. Bach and Handel wrote no such songs but devoted themselves, after the fashion of their time, to bigger things—cantatas, operas, oratorios, and passions. Their successors, Gluck, Haydn, Mozart, and Beethoven, did write a considerable number of *Lieder*; but unfortunately they, too, reserved their best melodies for their larger works. Hence it is no injustice to this period to admit only two of its songs to our limited collection.

Das Veilchen—The Violet. This is by far the best of the three dozen or more songs written by Mozart. Goethe's plaintive and dainty poem evidently interested him, and he took pains (as he did in the best pages of his operas) to adapt his music lovingly to the changing moods of the text —the story of the loving violet crushed by the foot of the beloved.

Adelaide. Beethoven was twenty-five years old when he composed this song. It became popular at once—so popular, indeed, that he was annoyed and sometimes wished he had never written it; just as Wagner used to be angered when he had to listen, for the thousandth time, to his *Lohengrin* or *Tannhäuser* march. *Adelaide,* nevertheless, remains by far the best of Beethoven's songs. From a strictly formal point of view it is a solo cantata in the old Italian sense of the word rather than a *Lied*; but that need not trouble anybody. The music always reflects the spirit of the poem, which Beethoven considered "heavenly"; the melody is charming, and no song written up to that time had had such an interesting and varied pianoforte part.

FRANZ SCHUBERT (1797–1828)

SCHUBERT was the first of the great masters who gave his very best in his *Lieder*, and for this reason he is justly regarded as the father of the art-song. He was the most spontaneous and inexhaustible melodist of all times and countries; and whereas the operatic arias of Rossini, Donizetti, and Bellini are now for the most part faded, because they were written to gratify a transient fashionable taste, Schubert's melodies, written simply for his own satisfaction, are as fresh and fragrant as on the day when they burst into bloom. The best of his songs have never been equalled, not only in melody, but in harmonic modulation, dramatic realism, and power to stir the emotions. Liszt confessed that they often moved him to tears; and many others are affected by them in the same way.

Der Erlkönig—The Erlking. Schubert was only seventeen when he wrote that beautiful song, *Margaret at the Spinning Wheel.* In the following year he composed what many judges consider the greatest of all songs, *The Erlking*, the 178th of his *Lieder.* Spaun relates that one afternoon he went with a friend to call on Schubert. They found him all aglow reading Goethe's ballad, *The Erlking*, aloud. He walked up and down the room several times, book in hand, then suddenly sat down and, as fast as his pen could travel, put the superb ballad on paper, nearly in its present form, though he subsequently made some changes. This ballad by the boy Schubert is as splendidly and realistically dramatic as anything Wagner wrote in his most mature years. The incessant galloping triplets in the piano part not only impersonate the horse but conjure up the storm. The coaxing Erlking, the terrified child, the soothing father, have all a language of their own, different from the narrative, and the singer must modify his tone and style accordingly. The dissonance of the child's shriek was something new, thrilling, terrible, epoch-making in music.

Der Wanderer—The Wanderer. This is another one of the early songs that reveal Schubert's genius full-fledged. Think of such a song being written in a paroxysm of inspiration in one evening, by a youth of nineteen! In popularity and merit *The Wanderer* is almost on a level with *The Erlking*.

Der Tod und das Mädchen—Death and the Maiden. No song ever written has so much genius and emotion condensed into such a few bars as this. Certainly there is none that conjures up a sombre mood with such simple means. "After the poor girl has begged the 'skeleton man' to pass her by because she is so young, how full of gloomy foreboding are the two bars leading over to the second speaker—Death! And while he asks her in soothing words not to dread him, since he has come not to punish but to let her sleep gently in his arms, his monotonous, cavernous tones and the strange modulations tell us his real intentions." Note the simple but wonderful modulations from the words "bin nicht wild" to "schlafen."

Du bist die Ruh—My Peace thou art. This song belongs to the same year (1823) as the famous cycle of the *Müller-Lieder.* It is simple and melodious—"one of the most spiritual flights in all song literature," as William Arms Fisher has aptly characterized it.

Horch, horch, die Lerch—Hark, hark, the Lark. Schubert set to music verses by eighty-five different poets. Of his three Shaksperian songs the serenade, *Hark, hark, the Lark*, is the most famous, although *Who is Sylvia?* is also deservedly popular. The circumstances under which the serenade was written admirably illustrate the spontaneity of Schubert's genius. One afternoon, as he was sitting with some friends in the garden of a tavern near Vienna, he saw a volume of Shakspere on the table. He took it up and turned over the leaves till he came to *Hark, hark, the Lark* (in *Cymbeline*). After looking at it a few moments he exclaimed: "A lovely melody has come into my head; if I only had some music paper!" One of his friends drew a few staves on the back of a bill of fare, and Schubert, undisturbed by the tavern noises, jotted down his delightful song.

Das Wirthshaus—The Inn (Cemetery). Schubert once wrote in his diary that those of his songs which were born of sorrow alone, appeared to give the world the most satisfaction. In the autumn of 1827, a year before his death, he was for a time unusually depressed and melancholy. One day he said to his friend Spaun: "Come to Schober's to-day. I 'll sing you a cycle of weird songs. They have affected me more deeply than any others I have written." When the time came, he sang his new cycle, *The Winter Journey*. His friends were dumfounded by the gloomy mood of these songs, and at first did not quite appreciate them. But Schubert said: "I like these songs better than any of the others I have written, and you will come to like them too." He was right, for they all soon became enthusiastic over these melancholy songs, which prove once more that the best in art is usually the ineffably sad. Ineffably sad is *Das Wirthshaus*, the twenty-first of this cycle of twenty-four songs; and what makes this the more remarkable is that it is written in a major key. It must be played with deep expression, and poignant but not exaggerated accents.

Aufenthalt—My Abode. The last fourteen songs composed by Schubert were issued in a collection to which the publisher gave the appropriate title of "Swansong." It includes seven of his very best *Lieder*, beside the most popular of them all, the *Serenade*, "Leise flehen meine Lieder," which is not so poor as its excessive popularity might lead one to suppose. But the one following it—*Aufenthalt*—is much better. It is one of those songs which made Rubinstein exclaim rapturously: "Once more and a thousand times more, Bach, Beethoven, and Schubert are the three highest pinnacles of music." Vocalists who know how to build up a climax will delight in the high G near the close; and the pianist has a part as superbly energetic as in *The Erlking*. The bass is delightfully melodious, in an imitative way, and the interludes are of incomparable beauty and eloquence.

Der Doppelgänger—My Phantom Double. This, the last but one of Schubert's songs, makes his death at the early age of thirty-one seem the greatest calamity that ever occurred in the realm of music. It is not only one of the most wonderful songs ever written, but it opens up a new epoch in the history of the *Lied*. In its vocal recitative, its weird, expressive harmonies, the close correspondence of the music with the text, word by word, it anticipates nearly everything that Schumann, Liszt, Grieg, and the other great songwriters did after him. "The singer's task here is, first of all, to represent and interpret the poet, while to the pianist are intrusted chords as weird, as thrilling, as modern, as those which accompany the music of Erda and Klingsor in Wagner's *Siegfried* and *Parsifal*. . . . It is the most thrilling, the most dramatic of all lyrics, and in penning it Schubert helped to originate the music of the future." When it was written Wagner was a boy of fifteen.

FRÉDÉRIC CHOPIN (1809–1849)

THE people of Poland sing many songs which they attribute to Chopin. The only ones, however, which are certainly known to be his are contained in the collection of seventeen published after his death as Opus 74. Rubinstein called Chopin "the soul of the pianoforte," and it is true that he devoted himself to that instrument almost exclusively. These songs are, however, a notable exception. Amateurs will find most of them full of charm. They were written in the years 1824 to 1844, and they are for the most part as quaintly exotic and orchidean as his mazurkas.

Meine Freuden—My Delight. This is one of the six Chopin songs of which Liszt made such free and poetic transcriptions for the pianoforte alone. It is even more charming in its simpler, yet equally impassioned, original form. The rapture of a kiss has never been more ecstatically portrayed than in this song about the lips and their uses.

Zwei Leichen—The Parted Lovers. A more dismal text has perhaps never been set to music than this poem about two corpses—one that of a soldier, dying in the forest amid the croaking of crows and the howling of wolves; the other that of his sweetheart, dying at the same time in the town to the booming sound of the church bell. It is no disparagement to the music in this case to say that it does not quite equal the poem in grewsomeness. It is simply melancholy and melodious.

ROBERT SCHUMANN (1810–1856)

LOVE was the chief inspiration of Schumann's songs, as it has been of so many other works of art. In the year of his marriage (1840) he wrote more than a hundred *Lieder*, whereas before that he had devoted himself to the pianoforte alone. He wrote to his fiancée Clara Wieck that he "laughed and wept for joy" in composing these songs; and in other letters: "Without such a bride no one could write such music." "I could sing myself to death, like a nightingale." It is under such conditions that immortal songs are created. Unfortunately, Schumann did not, after 1840, write any more songs till nine years later, when the brain disease to which he succumbed in 1856 had already begun to reduce his genius to mere talent and routine. This explains why his later songs are not equal to the earlier ones. The four here presented rank with the best ever written.

Widmung—Dedication. This is one of the most popular of the Schumann songs. Through an accidental oversight it was omitted from the list of "starred" songs in *Songs and Song Writers*; but it is one of the best of all—full of that buoyant rhythmic swing and animation so characteristic of Schumann.

Die Lotosblume — The Lotus Flower. This, like *Widmung*, belongs to the group of twenty-six songs called "Myrtle Wreath" and dedicated by the composer to "his beloved bride." Heine's poem about the lotus flower which dreads the scorching sun and loves the pale moon is so exquisitely perfect that to add music to it seems like painting the lily. But when you hear Schumann's music, you realize that Wagner was right in maintaining that poetry and music are more potent in combination than singly.

Waldesgespräch—In the Forest. The legend of the beautiful sorceress Loreley (which was invented by Brentano in 1800) is known to most persons through Heine's poem wherein she is represented as a golden-haired maiden sitting on a rock overhanging the Rhine and luring the fisherman to destruction by her singing (see Liszt's song in this collection). Eichendorff's poem, used by Schumann, makes her roam the forest on horseback and inform the knight who wooes her, before he recognizes her as the witch, that he shall never more get out of the forest alive. The mystic and grewsome suggestiveness of such a scene appealed irresistibly to the romantic temperament of the German Schumann and enabled him to reproduce its spirit admirably in his music. As sung by Lilli Lehmann, or Lillian Nordica, this song sends the cold shivers down one's back.

Ich grolle nicht—I'll not complain. Of Schumann's two hundred and forty-five songs this is at once the most popular and the most inspired. It forms number six of *Dichterliebe*, a group of sixteen songs from Heine's *Buch der Lieder*. In these songs the union of the music with the poems is so intimate that, as has been aptly said, "it is sometimes impossible to rid ourselves of the impression that they are the work of one man."

This is particularly so in the case of *Ich grolle nicht*—a superbly effective outburst of woe and despair which proves once more that the best in art is the ineffably sad.

FRANZ LISZT (1811–1886)

WITH the exception of opera and chamber-music, there is no branch of the divine art in which Liszt did not do original—in fact, epoch-making—work. Next to this versatility his most remarkable trait is his cosmopolitanism. He was equally at home in Paris, Weimar, Budapest, and Rome; a wanderer, like the gypsies whose melodies he adopted. Hungarian, German, Italian, and French traits and influences can be traced in his music; but all have suffered

"a sea-change
Into something rich and strange;"

—so rich and strange that it has taken the world half a century to learn to appreciate this new art; the difficulty being increased by the fact that his forms were novel as well as his harmonies; and new forms and harmonies are but slowly accepted in music. Of his songs, half a dozen are French, and two of them, *Isten Veled* and *The Three Gypsies*, are Hungarian. The other fifty-one were written to German poems, and have the romantic and emotional qualities of German *Lieder*.

Die Lorelei—The Loreley. Before Liszt set Heine's famous poem to music the Germans had always sung it to Silcher's simple tune, which has the character of a genuine folk-song. It is a pretty melody and adapts itself well enough to the general mood of the poem. But it is always the same, in all the successive stanzas—the same whether the poet talks about his own melancholy mood, or about the calmly flowing Rhine at sunset, or about the maiden on the rock above, combing her golden hair, or about the enchanting lay she sings,

or about the wild longing which seizes the fisherman in the boat below, or about his heedlessness of the dangerous rocks, and the turbulent waters which finally engulf him. Liszt, on the contrary, saw here the possibilities of a miniature music-drama in which the melody and the expressive harmonies *continually change with the text*, as in a Wagner opera. The result is one of the most enchantingly realistic and dramatic songs in existence, replete with seductive melody, and agitated by a storm worthy of the composer of the *Flying Dutchman*. But let no bungling singer or pianist attempt it!

Der König von Thule—The King of Thule. Like the *Loreley*, this famous and effective ballad was composed by Liszt in 1841, on the quiet Rhine island Nonnenwerth, in the romantic region near the seven peaks of the Siebengebirge. It has all the beauty and eloquence of a Chopin ballad, with the added advantage of Goethe's emotional poetry. It occurs in his *Faust*.

Wanderers Nachtlied—Wanderer's Night Song. The charm of this song lies in its harmonies rather than its melody; but if the pianist is a genuine artist the effect is enchanting. Note the *molto tranquillo* and the *sotto voce* called for to express the lull in the tree-tops, when the breezes are at rest, the birds silent, and the nearness of death is suggested. Concerning the wonderful harmonies of this song, Dr. Hueffer has well said: "Particularly the modulation from G major back into the original E major, at the close of the piece, is of surprising beauty."

RICHARD WAGNER (1813–1883)

EVERYBODY knows that Wagner was a specialist of the opera, as Chopin was of the pianoforte. Yet he, too, wrote a few songs—ten in all. Four of them—*Dors, mon enfant, Attente, Mignonne*,

and *The Two Grenadiers*—were written in Paris (1839) as potboilers (he got about four dollars apiece for them!). In the following year he wrote *Der Tannenbaum*. The best of his songs, however, are *Träume* and *Im Treibhaus,* two of five which he composed in 1862. These two are studies to *Tristan and Isolde,* like the preliminary sketches which great artists make of their paintings and which sometimes surpass, in details, the paintings themselves.

Träume—Dreams. Singers who have never heard *Tristan and Isolde,* the most characteristic and inspired of Wagner's operas, will get, through this song, a glimpse into an entirely new world of harmonic delights—the thrilling love-music of what may be aptly called the German *Romeo and Juliet.*

ROBERT FRANZ (1815–1892)

SCHUMANN was the first who discovered the genius of Franz as a song-writer. "Were I to dwell on all the exquisite details in his songs," he wrote, "I should never come to an end." Manuel Garcia, the most eminent teacher in the nineteenth century of the best Italian method (Jenny Lind was one of his pupils), declared that of all German songs Franz's were the best adapted to the voice. Though usually of the declamatory order, they *can* be sung as smoothly as the *bel canto* of the Italians. The secret was indicated by Franz himself: "It is easy to sing my songs if the vocalist saturates himself with the poem and thus endeavors to reproduce the musical content." Liszt repeatedly referred to Franz as the best of the lyric composers. But the greatest compliment was paid to Franz by Wagner, in the days of his exile in Switzerland. When Franz visited him in 1857, he took him to his bookcase and showed him his collection of music. It consisted of some works of Bach and Beethoven and the songs of Franz—nothing more. He also sang some of the Franz songs for the composer in a very dramatic way, and to the end of his life had them sung frequently in his family circle at Bayreuth. This is the more remarkable, because Wagner, while worshipping the old masters, had little love for his contemporaries.

Bitte—Request. Ambros called this song "the prayer of a deep soul." It must be sung rather slowly, but with the religious fervor of a hymn —for it is a hymn to love, to a woman's dreamy, soulful black eyes.

> "*For where is any author in the world*
> *Teaches such beauty as a woman's eye?*"

An American woman, to whom Franz showed a picture of the wife he had just lost, while the tears were rolling down his cheeks, said to her companion : "Now I understand why his black-eyed song is so beautiful."

Für Musik—For Music. Mendelssohn (whose own songs are now so stale that none of them was deemed worthy of inclusion in this volume) once found fault with the songs of Franz because "the melody could not be detached from the piano part." As if that were not one of their greatest merits! Franz's songs are melodious not only in the vocal part but in every part of the "accompaniment." Harmony and melody became inseparable, as in the polyphonic works of Bach. Of the two hundred and seventy-nine songs written by Franz, none illustrates this peculiarity better than *Für Musik,* which is like a thicket in which a nightingale sings on every bush. The pianist must heed the directions: *il canto molto espressivo* —the melody to be brought out with deep feeling.

Widmung — Dedication. Another love-song, inspired, like *Bitte,* by a pair of eyes. "Oh, thank me not for these songs. They are yours, not mine. I read them in your eyes and simply copied them." This was one of Wagner's two favorites among Franz's songs.

Willkommen, mein Wald—Now welcome, my Wood! The majority of Franz's songs are slow and sad—*andantino* and *larghetto* being his favorite tempi. Of the lively and energetic ones *Willkommen, mein Wald* is a stirring example, with the exhilarating atmosphere of the forest. Oddly enough, Franz once remarked to a friend that he considered this one of his poor songs, and that he had hesitated to print it. Beethoven, in the same way, used to wish he could destroy his *Adelaide,* which is unquestionably the best of all his songs. These are eccentricities of genius.

Wonne der Wehmuth—Delight of Melancholy. Goethe was not the first poet to dwell on the delights of sadness. Fletcher wrote, long before him, "There's naught in this life sweet . . . but only melancholy"; and whole books have been written on "the ecstasy of woe." Milton coined the expression "melodious tear," and Franz's song is such a tear.

Es hat die Rose sich beklagt—The Rose complained. This has always been one of the most popular of Franz's songs, and deservedly so. If played with tenderness and delicacy the music is as fragrant as the rose it immortalizes. Use the pedal, and notice the exquisitely plaintive effect in the pianoforte part of the C following the word "beklagt."

PETER CORNELIUS (1824—1874)

CORNELIUS was an intimate friend of Liszt and Wagner. He composed several operas, one of which—*The Barber of Bagdad*—had considerable success, though its failure at Weimar so disgusted Liszt that he resigned his post as conductor. Some of the songs of Cornelius are admirable. Like Wagner, he wrote his own poems. He also published a volume of poems without music.

Ein Ton—The Monotone. This song is one of the greatest curiosities in all musical literature. The singer has only one tone throughout the forty-two bars of the composition, and the strangest thing about it is that very few persons realize this fact on hearing it the first time. But while the song is a monotone, it is anything but monotonous. So ingeniously varied is the piano part, and so interesting the harmonies, that the piece deserves to be classed with the mastersongs. Note that the poem suggests the peculiar treatment of the vocal part.

ANTON RUBINSTEIN (1829—1894)

RUBINSTEIN was one of the most fertile and original melodists of all time, and nowhere does the fount of his melody flow more freely than in his songs, most of which were written to German poems. Not a few of them are trivial and will share the fate of Mendelssohn's. But the best of them have a unique charm. Amateurs will find them easier to sing than most modern songs.

Der Asra—The Asra. Schubert himself might have been proud to have written this, one of the most truly vocal, original, and charming songs in existence. What a swing to the melody! and how quaint and exotic are its Oriental intervals at the words "welche sterben wenn sie lieben"—so appropriate to the romantic story of the Arabic slave, who grows paler every time he sees the princess, because he belongs to the tribe of the Asra, who die when they love.

Gelb rollt mir zu Füssen—Golden at my Feet. The quaint Oriental intervals which occur in *Der Asra* characterize also the whole group of Persian songs (Opus 34) which Rubinstein composed to twelve of Bodenstedt's *Songs of Mirza Schaffy*. The most spontaneous, buoyant, and popular of them is this love-song, sung on the banks of the river Kura.

JOHANNES BRAHMS (1833—1897)

EXPERTS are not agreed as to the rank of Brahms. All, however, admire his chamber-music and some of his songs. In Germany and England the songs of Brahms are at present almost as popular as Mendelssohn's were at one time; nor can it be denied that some of them, notably the three here presented, are very good, and likely to endure.

Wie bist du meine Königin— My Queen. There

is a languor and a sweetness in this song of ecstatic love that suggest the rich fragrance of a tuberose. In studying this and the other Brahms songs, remember that, as Mrs. Wodehouse has well said, in them the accompaniment stands in the same relation to the voice part as the pianoforte part stands to the violin in a sonata written for those two instruments.

Minnelied — Love Song. It may seem odd that the best two of Brahms's songs should have been inspired by poems of love, for he was never married; but love exercises its creative spell even over bachelor composers. The *Minnelied* (*Minne* is the old German word for *Liebe*, or *love*) seems to the editor the most inspired and delightful of Brahms's compositions.

Wie Melodien zieht es mir — A Thought like Music. Groth's poem seems to demand a musical setting, and Brahms has given it one which is both appropriate and beautiful.

ADOLF JENSEN (1837–1879)

ALTHOUGH Jensen wrote some admirable pianoforte pieces, he may nevertheless be classed with the song specialists, for the best products of his genius are to be found among his one hundred and sixty songs. In America he has never received the attention he deserves, but in Germany he is popular, and some of the experts rank him as high as Franz, or even higher. His idols were Schumann and Wagner.

Lehn' deine Wang' an meine Wang' — Press thy cheek against mine own. This is the first of his songs which Jensen considered good enough to print. It is a splendid setting of Heine's famous love-poem, full of emotion, with a touching melody and stirring voluptuous harmonies. Few songs are at the same time so good and so popular.

Wenn durch die Piazzetta — When through the Piazzetta. While *Press thy cheek* is one of those songs with which every one falls in love at first hearing, this and the following one are of the kind which must be studied with devotion before their ravishing beauty becomes apparent and haunts the memory. When his genius was in its full maturity, Jensen became enamoured of English poetry and he set to music seven poems by Burns, seven by Moore, four by Cunningham, six by Scott, and six by Tennyson. So anxious was he to preserve the spirit and fragrance of these poems that in composing them he consulted several translations beside the originals. He considered these, justly, the best of his lyrics, and referred to them, in 1877, as "my last and grandest excursion in the land of song."

Leis' rudern hier, mein Gondolier! — Row gently here, my Gondolier! Of the innumerable Venetian boat-songs this is surely the most delightful. Arnold Niggli, in his book on Jensen, writes regarding these two songs, that "in *When through the Piazzetta*, in which the guitar-like accompaniment emphasizes its character as a serenade, the singer's love ardor is touched by a breath of melancholy; while the second serenade, *Row gently here*, floats dreamily on the waters like the soft light of the moon."

PIOTR ILYITCH TCHAÏKOVSKY (1840–1893)

IN London concert halls the two most popular composers at the beginning of the twentieth century are Wagner and Tchaïkovsky. So far, however, Tchaïkovsky is known chiefly as a writer for the orchestra. Of his one hundred songs only a few have been brought forward, although there are many gems among them. Their day will come.

No poet has inspired so many first-class songs as Heinrich Heine. The highly concentrated feeling in his poems makes them specially suitable for musical setting. *Warum sind denn die Rosen so blass? — Why so pale are the roses?* is an excellent example. Note how the poet himself leads up to the splendid climax in the music, when the absence of the beloved is made responsible for all the sadness in nature and life.

Nur wer die Sehnsucht kennt—None but the lonely Heart. Though one of the earliest of Tchaïkovsky's compositions (Opus 6), this song displays the ripest musicianship, and is one of the best settings of Goethe's oft-composed poem. "Written with tears at his heart," as James Huneker says, "*Nur wer die Sehnsucht kennt* is fit to keep company with the best songs of Schubert, Schumann, Franz, and Brahms. In intensity of feeling and in the repressed tragic note this song has few peers. It is a microcosm of the whole Romantic movement."

Déception—Disappointment. With the possible exception of Germany, no country has so many of the fragrant wild flowers we call folk-songs as Russia. The majority are of a melancholy cast. Tchaïkovsky's *Disappointment* has the characteristics of a genuine Russian folk-song, and its sadness is intensified by the poignant harmonies with which the composer of the Pathetic Symphony knew how to express the "ecstasy of woe."

ANTONÍN DVOŘÁK (1841–1904)

THE engagement of Antonín Dvořák as director, for several years, of the National Conservatory of Music in New York, by Mrs. Jeannette M. Thurber, is a good illustration of the influence women have so often exerted on musical affairs; for it led to the composition of the greatest symphony and the finest chamber-music ever written in America. It is in the several branches of instrumental music that Dvořák has done his best work; yet some of his vocal pieces—notably his Gypsy Songs—are very beautiful too.

Als die alte Mutter—As my dear old Mother. Every one who has heard the slow movement of the *New World* symphony knows that Dvořák is a man of deep feeling. This song about the aged mother gives further proof of that fact; it doubtless owes some of its fervor to reminiscent filial devotion. Bohemian music is particularly rich and varied in its rhythms, and the rhythms of this song are difficult and need careful study.

JULES MASSENET (1842–)

FRANCE has produced no song specialists comparable to Schubert, Franz, or Jensen; and, while Gounod, Bizet, Saint-Saëns, Berlioz, and other masters wrote a considerable number of romances, they hardly ever put their best melodies into them, reserving these, as the Germans did before Schubert, for their operas and other large works. Massenet's fame, too, is based chiefly on his operas and choral works; yet he wrote several excellent songs.

Elégie—Elegy. Of all the songs ever written in France this is probably the best. It is one of the few Parisian productions to which one cannot apply Liszt's criticism that French *chansons* and *romances* lack the *Sehnsucht* and *Gemüth*— the sentimental yearning and romanticism that are essential to the genuine *Lied*. Massenet's *Elégie* is not only a beautiful "mélodie" as he calls it, but it has the true elegiac *Innigkeit*, or soulfulness. The piano part, also, is made exceptionally interesting by imitative touches; that is, bars in which it echoes the melody. These must be played with fervent expression.

EDVARD GRIEG (1843–1907)

JUST as every European country has its own picturesque national costumes and customs, so it has its peculiar folk-music, which an expert easily recognizes. Grieg's wonderful melodies have some of the rugged, sombre, irregular, abrupt qualities of Norwegian folk-song. But they are, with very few exceptions, of his own invention. Even more exotic and individual are his harmonies, which are as novel, daring, and fascinating as those of Schubert, Chopin, and Wagner. Grieg has, indeed, created the latest harmonic atmosphere in music. His harmonies are "caviare to the general," but musical epicures delight in their freshness and piquancy, their surprises, and their avoidance of commonplaces. Grieg's songs are like Wagner's operas inasmuch as they open up an entirely new world of musical enchantments.

Vom Monte Pincio—From Monte Pincio. The Pincio, in Rome, used to be known as the "hill of gardens." Here two thousand years ago were the famous gardens of the millionaire Lucullus, and many memories of mediæval events are associated with the place, too. At present it is a fashionable resort and drive, and in the evening, when there is music, it presents a gay scene. Björnson touches on the various points of view which occur to a poet's observant and reminiscent mind on a visit to this picturesque place; and Grieg's music, with a realistic art worthy of both Schubert and Liszt, reproduces all these aspects in his music—the glowing sunset, the swarming people, the domes of the city below, the mists calling up dim memories of the past and prophecies as to a future awakening of Rome to her former glory. Note how the opening chords conjure up the sunset mood; how the music grows funereal at the words "face of the dead"; note the echo-like sounds of the mountain horns; the fine contrast provided by the recurring gay melody (*vivo*); and many other exquisite details.

Mit einer Primula veris—The First Primrose. This is perhaps the best song for a first introduction to Grieg. Its ravishing melody enraptures the senses at a first hearing, and every one will agree that it is the loveliest of spring songs. All the tenderness of a flower, the fragrance of spring, the buoyancy of youth, are in this song of a lover who offers the first primrose of spring to his sweetheart in exchange for her heart.

Ein Schwan—A Swan. This is not only one of the most popular songs in modern concert halls, but is also one of the grandest ever composed. No one should attempt to sing it unless endowed with sufficient dramatic feeling to bring out the deeper meaning of Ibsen's poem, the varied expression, and, especially, the superb climax where the swan, after a life-long silence, sings at last. Grieg, in a letter to the editor, has called particular attention to the fact that the words "Ja da, da sangst du" should be sung "*sempre fortissimo,* if possible even with a *crescendo,* and by no means *diminuendo* and *piano.*"

An einem Bache—At the Brookside. When Grieg became acquainted, in 1880, with the poems of Vinje, he was "all aflame with enthusiasm," to use his own words, and in less than a fortnight he wrote a group of more than a dozen songs, to which this and the following one belong. In both of them we have Grieg at his very best, and in his most characteristic Norwegian mood. Here we come across melodic intervals and harmonic progressions so strange that at first they may seem to some persons almost like misprints; but after the ear has become habituated to them they assume an unearthly beauty. The charm of this original musical physiognomy grows on one like the expression of a face that indicates character as well as beauty.

Die alte Mutter—The Old Mother. A charming song of filial love and gratitude, which shows, like Dvořák's, that the romantic infatuation for a beautiful girl is not the only kind of love that inspires immortal music. Here the music is not so inseparably associated with the poem as in *Monte Pincio* and *A Swan;* but what a glorious melody, and what quaint, original harmonies!

Das Kind der Berge—The Mountain Maid. Grieg did not write much music in the last decade of the nineteenth century, because of his poor health. A few years ago, however, there appeared a group of eight songs, as Opus 67, under the general title of *The Mountain Maid.* It includes several gems, and the one selected for this volume is one of his most delightfully melodious and harmonically quaint and original *Lieder,* combining the freshness of youth with the depth of mature genius, and a touch of the Norwegian melancholy.

BENJAMIN GODARD (1849–1895)

JUST as, in Germany, Franz and Jensen wrote better songs than Mozart and Beethoven, so, in France, Godard and Delibes were better in this line than men of bigger calibre, like Berlioz, Gounod, and Saint-Saëns. Among the hundred or more songs written by Godard there is an unusual proportion of good ones,—songs that bear repetition well,—including the fine dramatic ballad *The Traveller* and the quaintly exotic *Arabian Song.*

Chanson de Florian—Florian's Song. The great popularity of this song is entirely deserved; for although it is somewhat less weighty than the other songs in this collection, it has a masterly melody, rising in "c'est mon ami" to a splendid emotional climax.

IGNACE JAN PADEREWSKI (1860–)

THE greatest of living pianists has heretofore devoted himself chiefly to composition for orchestra and pianoforte. His opera *Manru*, which has been produced so successfully in European and American cities, contains melodies (like "Einsam bin ich" and the Cradle Song) which would have made fine lyrical songs. His only *Lieder*, so far, are the six published as Opus 18. They deserve to be more widely known than they are at present.

Ach! die Qualen—Ah! the Torment! At first sight this seems almost like a cheerful song written to a plaintive, sentimental text; but if the singer and the player understand the Polish *rubato*, and the Polish *zal*,—a mixture of tenderness, agitation, humility, regret, resignation,— the composition will appear in its true light. It might be called a mazurka for the voice. The *meno mosso* part is enchantingly Paderewskian

EDWARD MacDOWELL (1861–1908)

EDWARD MacDOWELL has placed American music, so far as the art-song is concerned, on a level with the best that is done in Europe. Among his forty-five songs there are only a few (the earliest ones) that do not in every bar betray his genius for creating original melodies and harmonies. He is intensely modern, and "a regiment of soldiers could not make him write a stale melody or a platitudinous succession of chords, such as constitute the stock in trade of most song-writers." All singers will remember the day of their first acquaintance with MacDowell's songs as one of the most delightful in their experience. The best collection to begin with is the one entitled *Eight Songs*, which includes *The Robin sings in the Apple Tree*, *The West Wind croons in the Cedar Trees*, and others that have become favorites in the home and the concert hall.

The Sea. One advantage possessed by the MacDowell songs is that they were written for the most part to English or American poems, some of the best ones being by himself. His setting of W. D. Howells's *The Sea* has been aptly called by James Huneker "the strongest song of the sea since Schubert's *Am Meer.*" The rare poetic art with which Howells brings before our eyes the picture of the lover sailing away to sea, while the beloved stands on the shore and cries; followed by the picture of the wreck, and the lover lying asleep, far under, dead in his coral bed— is duplicated in the music, which shows a marvellous gift of emotional coloring in its harmonies, and is, in all other respects, a perfect song; the best, with the possible exception of his *Menie*, ever written in America. It is thanks to the kindness of the most famous of German music publishers, Breitkopf and Härtel, that it is possible to insert this copyrighted composition in this collection of mastersongs.

RICHARD STRAUSS (1864–)

RICHARD STRAUSS (who is not related to the "waltz-king") is the best-praised and the best-abused of contemporary German composers. The dispute is chiefly over his symphonic poems; his songs are admired by all. There are more than half a hundred, and while most of them are difficult to sing and play, they are worth careful study.

Ständchen—Serenade. Within the last few years this serenade has become one of the most popular pieces in our concert halls. If played by a nimble and intelligent pianist and sung by a vocalist of the dramatic type, it never fails to produce a fine effect, and to arouse a desire for further acquaintance with the works of this gifted young composer.

New York, March, 1902.

Henry T. Finck

THE MYSTERY OF SONG

The sound of music that is born of human breath,
Comes straighter from the soul than any strain
The hand alone can make.
                              As he sang—
Of what I know not, but the music touched
Each chord of being—I felt my secret life
Stand open to it, as the parched earth yawns
To drink the summer rain; and at the call
Of those refreshing waters, all my thought
Stir from its dark and secret depths, and burst
Into sweet, odorous flowers, and from their wells
Deep call to deep, and all the mystery
Of all that is, laid open.

                              ANON.

THE VIOLET
(DAS VEILCHEN)
(Composed in 1785)

(Original Key)

JOHANN WOLFGANG von GOETHE (1749-1832)

WOLFGANG AMADEUS MOZART
(1756 - 1791)

A vio-let blos-somed on the green With low-ly stem and bloom un-seen; It was a love-ly vio-let! A

Ein Veil-chen auf der Wie-se stand, ge-bückt in sich und un-be-kannt; es war ein her-zigs Veil-chen. Da

shep-herd maid-en came that way, With light-some step and as-pect gay, Came
kam ein' jun - ge Schä - fer - in mit leich - tem Schritt und mun - term Sinn da -

near, came near, came o'er the green with song.
her, da - her, die Wie - se her, und sang.

"Ah!" thought the vio - let,
Ach, denkt das Veil - chen,

"Might I be The fair-est flow-er on the lea, Ah! but
wär' ich nur die schön - ste Blu - me der Na - tur, ach! nur

for_ one brief hour! And might be plucked by that dear maid And
ein_ klei - nes Weil - chen, bis mich das Lieb - chen ab - ge-pflückt, und

gen - tly on her bo - som laid, Ah! but, ah! but a
an dem Bu - sen matt ge - drückt, ach! nur, ach!_ nur ein

few dear mo - ments long!" Ah! but a - las! the maid - en
Vier - tel - stünd-chen lang. Ach! a - ber ach! das Mäd - chen

passed, No eye up - on the vio - let cast, But crushed___
kam und nicht in Acht das Veil - chen nahm, er - trat___

ADELAÏDE

(Composed in 1795)

(Original Key)

FRIEDRICH von MATTHISSON (1761 - 1831)
Translated by John S. Dwight

LUDWIG van BEETHOVEN, Op. 46
(1770 - 1827)

Lone - ly wan - ders thy
Ein - sam wan - delt dein

friend in spring's green gar - den, Mild - ly stream - eth the mag-ic light a-
Freund im Früh - lings - gar - ten, mild vom lieb - lich-en Zau-ber-licht um-

gleams _____ thine _ im - age, thine _ im - age,
strahlt _____ dein _ Bild - niss, dein _ Bild - niss,

A - - de - la - i - de!
A - - de - la - i - de!

Eve - ning
A - bend - -

winds in the ten - der leaves are whisp'ring,
lüft - chen im zar - ten Lau - be flüs - tern,

Springs a blos-som from out my heart's cold ash - es, a blos-som from
ei - ne Blu - me der A-sche mei - nes Her - zens, der A - sche_

out my hearts ash - es; Clear - ly shin-ing, Clear - ly shin-ing on
mei - nes_ Her-zens; deut - lich schim-mert, deut - lich schim-mert auf

ev-'ry pur-ple pet-al, on ev'ry pur-ple pet-al: A - de-la-i - de,
je-dem Pur-pur-blätt-chen, auf je-dem Pur-pur-blätt-chen: A - de-la-i - de!

A - - - de-la-i - de, Clear-ly shin-ing on
A - - - de-la-i - de! deut-lich schim-mert auf

THE ERLKING
(DER ERLKÖNIG)
(Composed in 1815)

(*Original Key*)

JOHANN WOLFGANG von GOETHE (1749-1832)
Translated by Arthur Westbrook

FRANZ SCHUBERT, Op.1
(1797-1828)

Who rid - eth so late   through night and
Wer rei - tet so spät   durch Nacht und

wind? It is the fa-ther__ with his
Wind? Es ist der Va-ter mit sei - nem

child; He has the boy so safe in his
Kind; er hat den Kna - ben wohl in dem

arm, He holds him tight-ly, he holds him warm.
Arm, er fasst ihn si - cher, er hält ihn warm.

My son, in
Mein Sohn, was

father, my father, and see-est thou not the Erl-king's daugh-ters in
Va - ter, mein Va - ter, und siehst du nicht dort Erl - kö - nigs Töch - ter am

yon dim spot? My son, my son, I
dü - stern Ort? Mein Sohn, mein Sohn, ich

see, and I know 'Twas on - ly the old - en wil - low so gray.
seh' es ge - nau, es schei-nen die al - ten Wei - den so grau.

"I
„Ich

love thee so, thy beau - ty has rav - ished my sense; And, will - ing or
lie - be dich, mich reizt dei - ne schö - ne Ge - stalt, und bist du nicht

pp

not, I will car - ry thee hence." My fa - ther, my
wil - lig, so brauch' ich Ge - walt." Mein Va - ter, mein

fff

fa - ther, now grasps he my arm, The Erl - king has
Va - ter, jetzt fasst er mich an! Erl - kö - nig

sf *sf*

seized me, has done me harm! The
hat mir ein Leid's ge - than! Dem

sf *sf* *sf* *sf* *f*

THE WANDERER
(DER WANDERER)
(Composed in 1816)

GEORG FILIPP SCHMIDT(1766-1849)
Translated by Arthur Westbrook

(*Original Key, C# minor*)

FRANZ SCHUBERT, Op. 4, N⁰ 1
(1797 - 1828)

I come here from my moun tains lone,
Ich kom - me vom Ge - bir - ge her,

The vale is dim,
es dampft das Thal,

The sea doth moan, the sea doth
es braust das Meer, es braust das

moan.
Meer.

I wan-der on with pain and care,
Ich wand-le still, bin we - nig froh,

And ev-er asks my sigh-ing, "Where?" ev-er, "Where?" The
und im-mer fragt der Seuf-zer: Wo? im-mer Wo? Die

sun to me seems here so cold, The flow'rs are fad-ed and life is old. Their
Son-ne dünkt mich hier so kalt, die Blü-the welk, das Le-ben alt, und

speech doth seem but emp-ty sound, I feel a stran-ger ev'-ry-where.
was sie re-den, lee-rer Schall, ich bin ein Fremd-ling ü-ber-all.

Più mosso (Etwas geschwinder)

Where art thou, where art thou, My be-lov-ed land? In
Wo bist du, wo bist du, mein ge-lieb-tes Land? ge-

hope, I seek, yet nev- er
sucht, ge-ahnt, und nie ge-

Tempo, Adagio__ (*Wie anfangs, sehr langsam*)

art thou?
bist du?

I wan - der__
Ich wand - le__

on with pain and care,
still, bin we - nig froh,

And ev - er asks my sigh - ing,
und im - mer fragt der Seuf - zer:

"Where?" ev - er "Where?"
wo? im - mer wo?

In spir - it - voice the ans - wer comes:
Im Gei - ster-hauch tönt's mir zu - rück:

"There, where thou art not, there is thy rest!"
„Dort, wo du nicht bist, dort__ ist das Glück!"

DEATH AND THE MAIDEN
(DER TOD UND DAS MÄDCHEN)

(Composed in 1817)

MATTHIAS CLAUDIUS (1743-1815)
Translated by Arthur Westbrook

(Original Key, D minor)

FRANZ SCHUBERT, Op.7, Nº 3
(1797-1828)

(THE MAIDEN)
(DAS MÄDCHEN)

Pass on-ward, Oh! pass on-ward, Go,
Vor - ü - ber! ach, vor - ü - ber! *geh'*

wild and blood-less man! I am still young, A-
wil - der Kno - chen-mann! Ich bin noch jung, *geh;*

way then, and touch me not, I pray, Oh, touch me not, I pray.
lie - ber! und rüh - re mich nicht an, und rüh - re mich nicht an.

Tempo I

(DEATH) Give me thy hand, my fair and ten-der
(DER TOD) Gieb dei - ne Hand, du schön und zart Ge-

child, As friend I come, and not to __ chas - ten. Be of good
bild! bin Freund und kom - me nicht zu __ stra - fen. Sei gu - tes

cheer! I bring thee rest; To sleep with - in these fond arms has - -
Muths! ich bin nicht wild, sollst sanft in mei - nen Ar - men schla - -

ten!
fen!

MY PEACE THOU ART
(DU BIST DIE RUH)

(Composed in 1823)

(Original Key)

FRIEDRICH RÜCKERT (1788-1866)
Translated by Edward Rowland Sill

FRANZ SCHUBERT, Op.59, Nº 3
(1797-1828)

Words used by permission

Shut out all woe,＿ all＿less-er care and woe, I would thy
Treib' an - dern Schmerz＿ aus＿ die - ser＿ Brust! voll sei dies

hurt＿ and＿ heal - ing＿ know,＿ ·thy＿hurt and heal - ing
Herz＿ von dei - ner＿ Lust,＿ von＿ dei - ner＿

know.＿
Lust.＿

Clear light that on my soul hath shone, my
Dies Au - gen - zelt, von dei - nem Glanz al -

cresc.

soul hath shone,___ Still let_ it_ shine _____ from thee a -
*lein er - hellt,___ o_ füll' es_ ganz,_____ o_ füll' es_*

lone,___ Clear light that on my
ganz!___ Dies Au - gen - zelt, von

soul hath shone, my soul hath shone,___ Still let it_
*dei - nem Glanz al - lein er - hellt,___ o_ füll' es_*

shine_____ from thee a - lone._____
ganz, _____ o_ füll' es_ ganz!_____

*) According to the original edition ♮. The original M S has not been found.

HARK! HARK! THE LARK
(HORCH, HORCH, DIE LERCH!)

Serenade from "Cymbeline"

WILLIAM SHAKESPEARE (1564-1616)
German of first verse by A.W. Schlegel
Second and third German verses added by Fr. Reil, and
Translated by Isabella G. Parker

(Composed in 1826)

(Original Key)

FRANZ SCHUBERT (Posthumous)
(1797-1828)

1. Hark! hark! the lark at heav'n's gate sings, And Phoe - bus 'gins___ to
2. Through all the si - lent, love - ly night The star - ry hosts___ on
3. If this doth not a - wak - en thee, When love - songs, for___ thy

1. *Horch, horch, die Lerch' im Ae - ther blau! und Phö - bus, neu er -*
2. *Wenn schon die lie - be gan - ze Nacht der Ster - ne lich - tes*
3. *Und wenn dich al - les das nicht weckt, so wer - de durch___ den*

winking Mary-buds begin___ To ope their gold-en
thou wilt wake,_ their light to greet:_Come, ope thy star-ry
Love thee to___ thy win - dow brings, Well knows he:_ ope___ thine

Rin - gel - blu - me Knos - pe schleusst die gold' - nen Aeug - lein
auch dein Au - gen - stern sie grüsst,_Er - wach! Sie war - ten
oft sie dich___ an's Fen - ster trieb,_ das weiss sie, d'rum___ steh'

eyes, With ev - 'ry thing___ that pret - ty bin, My
eyes! Since thou so star - like art, so sweet, My
eyes, And love thy sing - er while he sings! My

auf; mit al - lem, was___ da rei - zend ist_ du
drauf, weil du doch gar___ so rei - zend bist; du
auf, und ha - be dei - nen Sän - ger lieb, du

THE INN
(DAS WIRTHSHAUS)

(Composed in 1828)

(*Original Key*)

WILHELM MÜLLER (1794 - 1827)
Translated by Alexander Blaess

FRANZ SCHUBERT, Op.89, № 21
(1797 - 1828)

death am I ex-haust - ed with grief and pain a-cute.
matt zum Nie-der-sin - ken, bin tödt-lich schwer ver-letzt.

Thou
O

inn, of pit-y bar-ren, yet turnst thou me a-way? Then on, my staff e'er faith-ful, till
un-barm-herz'-ge Schen-ke, doch wei-sest du mich ab? Nun wei-ter denn, nur wei-ter, mein

cresc.   *p*

death my care al-lay, Then on, my staff e'er faith-ful, till
treu-er Wan-der-stab, nun wei-ter denn, nur wei-ter, mein

cresc.

death my care al-lay.
treu-er Wan-der-stab!

MY ABODE
(AUFENTHALT)

(Composed in 1828)

LUDWIG RELLSTAB (1799-1860)
Translated by Louis C. Elson

Original Key, E Minor)

FRANZ SCHUBERT
"Schwanengesang," No 5
(1797-1828)

Not too quickly, yet with force (*Nicht zu geschwind, doch kräftig*)

PIANO

Swift rush-ing stream, loud moaning wood, Rockbleak and scarred, my
Rau-schen-der Strom, *brau-sen-der Wald,* *star-ren-der Fels, mein*

wild a - bode, Swift rush-ing stream, loud moan-ing wood,— Rock bleak and
Auf - ent - halt, *rau-schen-der Strom,_* *brau-sen-der Wald,_* *star - ren - der*

scarred, my wild a - bode.
Fels, mein Auf - ent - halt.

Bil - lows on bil - lows chase o'er o - cean's breast. So too are flow - ing my
Wie sich die Wel - le an Wel - le reiht, flie - ssen die Thrä - nen mir

tears without rest, so too are flow - ing my tears, my
e - wig er - neut, flie - ssen die Thrä - nen mir e - wig,

tears with-out rest, so too are flow-ing my tears with-out rest.
e - wig er - neut, flie - ssen die Thrä-nen mir e - wig er - neut.

cresc.

f

decresc.

Winds o'er the tree-tops are nev-er at peace, My heart's wild throbbing, like
Hoch in den Kro-nen wo-gend sich's regt, so un-auf-hör-lich mein

ben marcato

them, will not cease, Winds o'er the tree-tops are nev-er at peace, My
Her-ze schlägt, hoch in den Kro-nen wo-gend sich's regt, so

mf

heart's wild throb-bing, like them, will not cease, The wild, wild throbs of my
un-auf-hör-lich mein Her-ze schlägt, so un-auf-hör-lich mein

heart___ will not cease. And
Her-___-ze schlägt. Und

p

Swift rush-ing stream, loud moan-ing wood, Rock bleak and scarred, my wild a-
Rau - schen-der Strom, *brau-sen - der Wald,* *star-ren - der Fels,* *mein Auf-ent-*

bode, Swift rush - ing stream, loud moan-ing wood, Rock bleak and scarred,____
halt, *rau-schen - der Strom,* *brau-sen - der Wald,* *star-ren - der Fels,____*

____ swift rush-ing stream,____ loud____ moan-ing wood, my
____ *rau - schen-der Strom,____* *brau - - sen-der Wald,* *mein*

wild a - bode.____
Auf - ent - halt.____

MY PHANTOM DOUBLE
(DER DOPPELGÄNGER)

(Composed in 1828)

(Original Key)

HEINRICH HEINE (1799-1856)
Translated by Arthur Westbrook

FRANZ SCHUBERT,
"Schwanengesang," N⁰ 13
(1797-1828)

Still is the night o'er roof-tree and stee-ple;
Still ist die Nacht, es ru-hen die Gas-sen,

With-in this dwell-ing lived my treasure rare.
in die-sem Hau-se wohn-te mein Schatz;

Long since she left this town and peo-ple,
sie hat schon längst die Stadt ver-las-sen,

But still stands the house on the self - same square.
doch steht noch das Haus auf dem - sel - ben Platz.

Here stands, too, a man; towards heav - en he ga - zes, His hands he
Da steht auch ein Mensch und starrt in die Hö - he, und ringt die

wring-eth in wild - est de-spair;___ I___ shud - der,
Hän - de vor Schmer - zens-ge-walt;___ mir___ graust es,

when now his face he rais - es— The moon-light shows me mine own self is
wenn ich sein Ant - litz se - he— der Mond zeigt mir mei - ne eig' - ne Ge-

MY DELIGHT
(MEINE FREUDEN)

(Composed in 1837)

(Original Key)

ADAM MICKIEWICZ (1798–1855)
Translated by Nathan Haskell Dole

FRÉDÉRIC CHOPIN
(1809–1849)

When first the mag - ic of thy dear voice
Wenn du, Ge - lieb - te, nur be -ginnst zu

calls me, I am en - rap - tured; a won-drous charm en - thrals me!
re - den, bin ich ge - fan - gen mit tau - send Zau - ber - fä - den!

THE PARTED LOVERS
(ZWEI LEICHEN)
(Composed in 1845)

(Original Key, D minor)

BOGDAN ZALESKI (1802-1886)
Translated by NATHAN HASKELL DOLE

FRÉDÉRIC CHOPIN
(1809-1849)

1. Two fond young lov-ers, tho' faith-ful, tho' true-heart-ed,
1. Zwei die sich lieb-ten, die durf-ten's nicht ge-ste-hen,

Were kept from meet-ing, were from each o-ther part-ed.
muss-ten sich mei-den und von ein-an-der ge-hen.

Years swift-ly glid-ed by; still their love each cher-ished;
Jah-re ver-gin-gen, sah'n sich nie-mals wie-der,

Both came at last to_ die, All_ their sweet hopes per-ished!
leg-ten sich end-lich beid' zu ster-ben nie-der.

55

DEDICATION
(WIDMUNG)

(Composed in 1840)

(Original Key, A♭)

FRIEDRICH RÜCKERT (1788 - 1866)
Translated by Alexander Blaess

ROBERT SCHUMANN, Op. 25, N⁰ 1
(1810 - 1856)

Thou art my life, my soul and heart, Thou both my joy and sad-ness art, Thou art my heav'n, my match-less lov-er, The world of bliss where-in I

Du mei-ne See - le, du mein Herz, du mei-ne Wonn', o du mein Schmerz. du mei-ne Welt, in der ich le - be, mein Him-mel du, da-rein ich

THE LOTUS FLOWER
(DIE LOTOSBLUME)

(Composed in 1840)

HEINRICH HEINE (1799 - 1856)
Translated by Arthur Westbrook

(Original Key)

ROBERT SCHUMANN, Op. 25, No 7

(1810 - 1856)

Larghetto *(Ziemlich langsam)*

The Lo - tus flow'r doth lan - guish
Die Lo - tos - blu - me äng - stigt

Un - der the sun's fierce light,
sich vor der Son - ne Pracht,

With droop - ing head she wait - eth, She
und mit ge - senk - tem Haup - te er -

dream - i - ly waits for the night.
war tet sie träu - mend die Nacht.

The moon is her true lov - er, He
Der Mond, der ist ihr Buh - le, er

wakes her with fond em - brace;
weckt sie mit sei - nem Licht,

For him she glad - ly un - veil - eth Her
und ihm ent - schlei - ert sie freund - lich ihr

IN THE FOREST
(WALDESGESPRÄCH)

(Composed in 1840)

(Original Key)

JOSEPH von EICHENDORFF (1788-1857)
Translated by Alexander Blaess

ROBERT SCHUMANN, Op.39, №3
(1810-1856)

bride!" / heim!"   "Man's plead-ing way and lur - ing
"Gross ist der Män - ner Trug___ und

kiss / List,   Con - ceal de - ceit and ar - ti-
vor Schmerz mein Herz ge - bro - -chen

fice. / ist,   Know'st not my pale and heart - worn face? Oh,
wohl irrt das Wald - horn her___ und hin, o

flee!___ / flieh'!___   Oh, flee___ from this ac-curs-ed place!"
o flieh'!___ du weisst nicht, wer ich bin."

I'LL NOT COMPLAIN
(ICH GROLLE NICHT)

(Composed in 1840)

(Original Key)

HEINRICH HEINE (1799-1856)
Translated by John S. Dwight

ROBERT SCHUMANN, Op.48, No.7
(1810-1856)

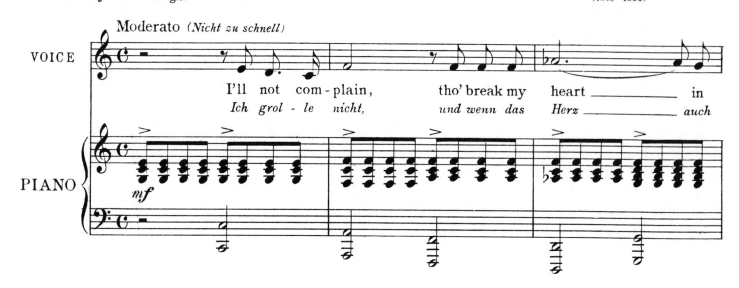

THE LORELEY
(DIE LORELEI)
(Composed in 1841)

(Original Key)

HEINRICH HEINE (1799-1856)
Translated by Arthur Westbrook

FRANZ LISZT
(1811-1886)

Moderato Non strascinando *(Nicht schleppend)*

PIANO

mf

Parlando
p (Gesprochen)

I know not what it be-to-kens That I such sad-ness, such sad-ness
Ich weiss nicht, was soll's be-deu-ten, dass ich so trau-rig, so trau-rig

p

know;
bin.

Allegretto

p

A le-gend of
Ein Mär-chen aus

p

by-gone a-ges
al-ten Zei-ten,

So haunts me, nor will it go, So haunts me, nor___
das kommt mir nicht aus dem Sinn, das kommt mir nicht___

poco rit.

poco rit.

THE KING OF THULE
(DER KÖNIG VON THULE)

(From "Faust")

(Composed in 1841)

JOHANN WOLFGANG von GOETHE (1749-1832)
Translated by Arthur Westbrook

(Original Key, F Minor)

FRANZ LISZT
(1811-1886)

Then closed his eyes, ne'er to o - - - pen,
Die Au - gen thä - ten ihm sin - - - ken.

And nev - er a - gain drank he,
Trank nie___ ei - nen Trop - fen mehr,

nev - er a - gain drank he.
trank nie ei - nen Trop - fen mehr.

WANDERER'S NIGHT SONG
(WANDERERS NACHTLIED)
(Composed in 1848)

(Original Key, E)

JOHANN WOLFGANG von GOETHE (1749-1832)
Translated by Arthur Westbrook

FRANZ LISZT
(1811-1886)

DREAMS
(TRÄUME)

Study for "Tristan and Isolde", Composed in 1862

(Original Key)

MATHILDE WESENDONCK
Translated by Isabella G. Parker

RICHARD WAGNER
(1813-1883)

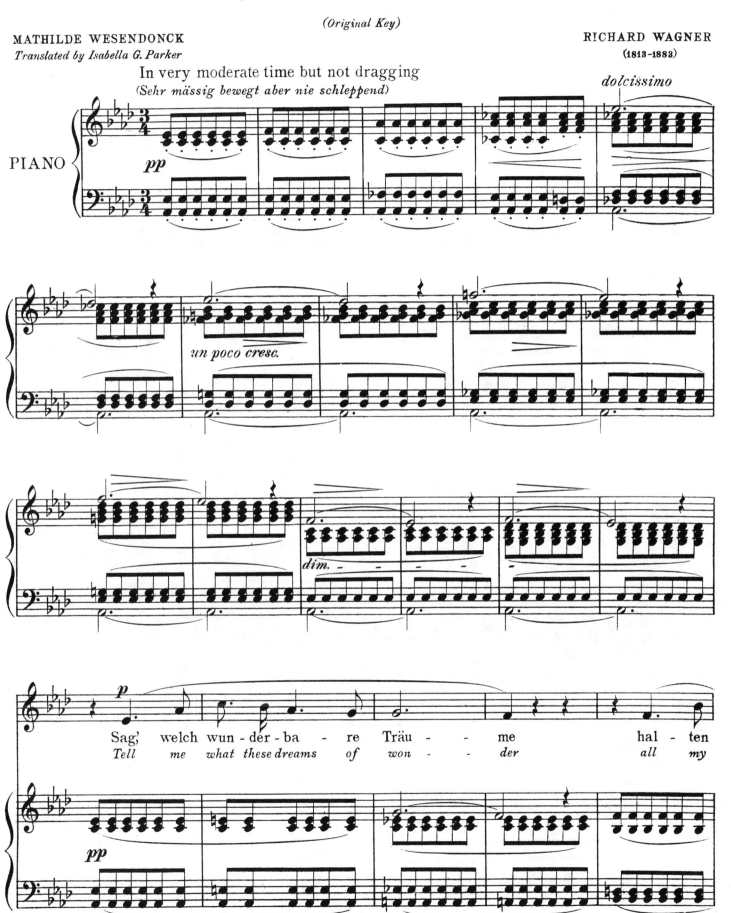

Sag', welch wun - der - ba - - re Träu - - me hal - ten
Tell me what these dreams of won - - der all my

mei-nen Sinn um-fan - - gen, dass sie nicht wie lee - re
soul in bonds en - chain - - ing, *Not like bub-bles burst a -*

Schäu - me sind in ö - des Nichts ver-gan-gen? Träu -
sun - der Leav-ing naught but foam re - main - ing? *Vi -*

me die in je - der Stun-de, je-dem Ta-ge schö - ner blüh'n und mit ih - rer
sions ev - er bright-er grow-ing Ev - 'ry day and ev - 'ry hour With a heaven-born

Him-mels-kun - de se - lig durchs Ge-mü - the ziehn? Träu -
lus - tre glow - ing Might - y in their ho - ly power. *Vi -*

To Joseph Fischhof

REQUEST
(BITTE)
(Original Key)

NIKOLAUS LENAU (1802-1850)
a) *Translated by Arthur Westbrook*
b) Translated by J.B. Johnson.

ROBERT FRANZ, Op. 9, N⁰ 3
(1815-1892)

Take, now, with thy som - bre mag - ic From my
Nimm mit dei - nem Zau - ber - dun - kel die - se
With thy pow'r of blest en - chant - ment, Take me

sight this world a - way, That a - lone thou
Welt von hin - nen mir, dass du ü - ber
from this world a - way; Rule my life and

may'st for - ev - er O'er my life ex - tend thy sway.
mei - nem Le - ben ein - sam schwe - best für und für.
rule for - ev - er, Thee a - lone will I o - bey.

To Frl. Louise von Platen

FOR MUSIC
(FÜR MUSIK)

(Original Key)

EMANUEL von GEIBEL (1815 - 1884)
Translated by Diana V. Ashton

ROBERT FRANZ, Op.10, No.1
(1815-1892)

Seeks my soul thy spir - it, Ha-ven, oh,___ how blest.___
steu - ert mei - ne See - le Dei-ner See - le zu.

Take my heart's de - vo - tion, Thine it is a - lone!___
*Die sich dir er - ge - ben, nimm sie ganz da - hin!*___

Ah, thou know'st that nev - er I have been my own, have been my own.
Ach, du weisst, dass nim - mer ich mein ei - gen bin, mein ei - gen bin.

To Frl. Hermine Haller

DEDICATION
(WIDMUNG)

(Original Key)

WOLFGANG MÜLLER (1816-1873)
Translated by Arthur Westbrook

ROBERT FRANZ, Op. 14, Nº 1
(1815-1892)

Oh, thank me not for what I sing thee; Thine are the
O dan - ke nicht für die - se Lie - der, *mir ziemt es*

songs, no gift of mine. Thou gav'st them me;___ I but re-
dank - bar Dir zu sein; *Du gabst sie mir,___* *ich ge - be*

turn thee what is and ev - er will be thine.
wie - der, was jetzt und einst und e - wig Dein.

Thine were they ev - 'ry one for - ev - er. The light___ which
Dein sind sie al - le ja ge - we - sen. Aus Dei - ner

in thy dear eyes shone Tru - ly hath taught me how___ to
lie - ben Au - gen Licht hab' ich sie treu - lich ab - ge -

read them; Dost thou not know___ they are___ thine own,___
le - sen, kennst Du die eig - nen Lie - der nicht?___

Dost thou not know___ they are___ thine own?___
kennst Du die eig - nen Lie - der nicht?___

NOW WELCOME, MY WOOD!

(WILLKOMMEN, MEIN WALD!)

OTTO ROQUETTE (1824–)
Translated by Elisabeth Rücker

(Original Key)

ROBERT FRANZ, Op.21, Nº 1
(1815 - 1892)

Now wel - come, my wood,____ thou green____ sha - dy
Will - kom - men, mein Wald,____ grün - schat - ti - ges

home!____ Thro' the branch - es now peals forth thy wel - com - ing
Haus!____ durch die Wip - fel schon hallt mir dein grü - ssend Ge-

tone.____ How glad - ly I breathe the fresh life - giv - ing
braus. Wie trink' ich in Zü - gen mich frisch und ge-

DELIGHT OF MELANCHOLY
(WONNE DER WEHMUTH)

(Original Key)

JOHANN WOLFGANG von GOETHE (1749-1832)
Translated by Arthur Westbrook

ROBERT FRANZ, Op. 33, No 1
(1815-1892)

Dry ye not, dry ye not, Tears of a love nev-er dy-ing! Ah! on-ly to eyes half dried from their

Trock - net nicht, trock - net nicht, Thrä - nen der e - wi - gen Lie - be! Ach nur dem halb - ge - trock - ne - ten

weep - ing How bar - ren, how dead the world still must seem! _____
Au - ge wie ö - de, wie todt die Welt ihm er - scheint! _____

Dry ye not, _____ dry ye not, _____
Trock - net nicht, _____ trock - net nicht, _____

Tears of un - for - tu - nate lov - ing! _____
Thrä - nen un - glück - li - cher Lie - be! _____

THE ROSE COMPLAINED
(ES HAT DIE ROSE SICH BEKLAGT)

FRIEDRICH von BODENSTEDT (1819-1892)
(From the Persian of Mirza Schaffy)

Translated by George L. Osgood

(Original Key)

ROBERT FRANZ, Op. 42, No 5
(1815-1892)

The rose com-plain'd with hang-ing head, Her fra-grance all too soon was go-ing, Which spring had lav-ish'd sweet and ver-nal!

Es hat die Ro-se sich be-klagt, dass gar zu schnell der Duft ver-ge-he den ihr der Lenz ge-ge-ben ha-be,

THE MONOTONE
(EIN TON)

(Original Key)

Translated by C. Hugo Laubach

Words and Music by
PETER CORNELIUS, Op.3, N̥o 3
(1824-1874)

Is it the ten-der mon-o-tone Of church-bell
ist es des Glöck-leins trü-ber Klang, der dir ge-

which for thee made moan? Lo, still it comes, so full, so
folgt den Weg ent-lang? Mir klingt der Ton so voll und

clear, As though thy soul were float-ing near,_____
rein, als schlöss er dei-ne See-le ein,_____

As though with love and yearn-ing deep You sang my bit - ter pain to
als stie - gest lie - bend nie - der Du und säng - est mei - nen Schmerz in

sleep! _____
Ruh! _____

THE ASRA
(DER ASRA)

(Original Key)

HEINRICH HEINE (1799-1856)
Translated by Arthur Westbrook

ANTON RUBINSTEIN, Op. 32, No 6
(1829 - 1894)

Ev-'ry day the won-drous love-ly Sul-tan's daugh-ter paced the gar-den,
Täg-lich ging die wun-der-schö-ne Sul-tans-toch-ter auf und nie-der

In the eve-ning near the foun-tain Where the foam-ing wa-ters whit-en.
um die A-bend-zeit am Spring-brunn, wo die wei-ssen Was-ser plät-schern;

Ev-'ry day the youth-ful slave stood In the eve-ning near the foun-tain,
täg-lich stand der jun-ge Skla-ve um die A-bend-zeit am Spring-brunn,

Where the foam-ing wa - ters whit - - en. Dai - ly grew he pale and
wo die wei - ssen Was - ser plät - - schern. Täg - lich ward er bleich und

pal - er, pale and pal - er. Till one eve - ning stept the Prin - cess
blei - cher, bleich und blei - cher. Ei - nes A - bends trat die Für - stin

To his side with hur - ried ques - tion. "Tell me, slave, thy name, thy coun - try!
auf ihn zu mit ra - schen Wor - ten: "Dei nen Na - men will ich wi - ssen,

Tell me of thy home and kin - dred!" And the slave re - plied: "Men
dei - ne Hei - math, dei - ne Sipp - schaft!" Und der Skla - ve sprach: "Ich

GOLDEN AT MY FEET
(GELB ROLLT MIR ZU FÜSSEN)

(Original Key)

FRIEDRICH von BODENSTEDT (1819-1892)
(from the Persian of Mirza Schaffy)
Translated by Arthur Westbrook

ANTON RUBINSTEIN, Op. 34, N.º 9
(1829-1894)

Gold - en at my feet rolls the Ku - ra in might,
Gelb rollt mir zu Fü - - ssen der brau-sen-de Kur,

Foam on the waves light - ly ri - - ding, Bright - ly
im tan-zen-den Wel - len - ge - trie - - be, hell

smiles all in sun - - shine, My heart laughs
lä - chelt die Son - - ne, mein Herz und die

light. _____ O would this were ev - er a - bid -
Flur. _____ *O,* *wenn es doch im - mer so blie -*

ing, O would this were ev - er a - bid - - - ing! _____
be, *O,* *wenn es doch im - mer so* *blie - - - - be!* _____

p   *mf*

2 Sparkles red in glass now our Geor-gi-an wine, The wine_ from my_
2 Roth fun - kelt im Glas der ka-che-ti-sche Wein, *es_____ füllt mir das*
3 Now_ sets the sun, swift-ly com-eth the night, My heart, like love's_
3 Die Son - ne geht un - ter, schon dun-kelt die Nacht, *doch mein Herz gleicht dem*

p

Love's hands soft glid - - ing. I____ drink from her eyes_____ The___
Glas__ mei - ne Lie - - be, und ich saug' mit dem Wein_____

stars so con - fid - ing, Still in deep-en-ing dark - ness Aye___
Ster - ne der Lie - - be, flammt in tief - sten Dun - - kel in___

light____ down__ in mine._____ O would this were ev - er a -
ih - re Bli - cke ein._____ O, wenn es doch im - mer so
glis - - tens__ more bright._____
hell - - ster Pracht._____

bid - ing, O would this were ev-er a - bid - - ing!
blie - be, O, wenn es doch im-mer so blie - - be!

MY QUEEN
(WIE BIST DU MEINE KÖNIGIN)

(Composed in 1864)

(Original Key)

G.F. DAUMER (1800-1875)
Translated by Arthur Westbrook

JOHANNES BRAHMS, Op.32, Nº 9
(1833-1897)

Ah, sweet my love, my gra-cious queen! As now, I've e'er thy sub-ject
Wie bist du mei - ne Kö - ni - gin, durch sanf - te Gü - te won - ne-

been.— Dost thou but smile, then all a - round sweet Spring is smil - ing.
voll:— Du läch - le nur, Lenz - düf - te weh'n durch mein Ge - mü - the

Thou my queen, thou my queen.
won - ne - voll, won - ne - voll!

Fresh is the bloom the ro - ses
Frisch auf - ge - blüh - ter Ro - sen

wear, Yet can it not with thine com-pare. Fair-est of
Glanz, ver-gleich ich ihn den dei - ni -gen? Ach, ü - ber

flow'rs thou bring-est joy my soul en-tranc - ing. Thou my
al - les was da blüht, is dei - ne Blü - the won - ne -

queen, thou my queen.
voll, won - ne - voll.

Tho' I might roam in des-erts drear, All would be changed should'st thou ap-
Durch to - dte Wü - sten wan-dle hin, und grü - ne Schat - ten brei-ten

pear, Fra-grance and sweet re-fresh-ing shade Thou___ bring'st me
sich, ob fürch-ter - li - che Schwü-le dort ohn'___ En - de

ev - er, Thou my queen, thou my
brü - te, won - ne - voll, won - ne -

LOVE SONG
(MINNELIED)
(Composed in 1877)

(Original Key)

H. HÖLTY (1828-1887)
Translated by Arthur Westbrook

JOHANNES BRAHMS, Op.71, No 5
(1833-1897)

Bright-er is the bloom-ing Spring, Green-er are its bow-
Rö - ther blü - hen Thal und Au, grü - ner wird der Ra -

- ers, When, with ten - der fin - gers' touch She doth gath - er
- sen, wo die Fin - ger mei - ner Frau Mai - en - blu - men

flow-ers: But for thee all joy were dead, All earth's
la - sen. Oh - ne sie ist al - les todt, welk sind

bright-ness fa - ded. E'en the glow of eve-ning sky Were for
Blüt' und Kräu - ter; und kein Früh - lings - a - bend - roth dünkt mir

me o'er-shad-ed.
schön und hei - ter.

Dear-est sov - 'reign of my
Trau - te, min - nig - li - che

heart, Leave, oh! leave me nev - er, Bloom sweet blos - soms of thy
Frau, wol - lest nim - mer flie - hen, dass mein Herz, gleich die - ser

love, In ____ my soul for ev - er, In my soul ____ for ev -
Au', mög' ____ in Won - ne ____ blü - hen, mög' in Won - ne blü -

er.
hen.

rit.

dolce   *dim.*   *p*

A THOUGHT LIKE MUSIC
(WIE MELODIEN ZIEHT ES MIR)
(Composed in 1889)

(Original Key, A)

KLAUS GROTH (1819-)
Translated by Isabella G. Parker.

JOHANNES BRAHMS, Op.105, № 1
(1833-1897)

A thought, like mu-sic,— hold-ing My
Wie Me-lo-di-en— zieht es mir

heart in soft con-trol, Like flow'rs of spring un-
lei-se durch den Sinn, Wie Früh-lings-blu-men

fold-ing, It thrill-eth through my soul,
blüht es und schwebt wie Duft da-hin,

It thrill - eth through my soul.
und schwebt wie Duft da - hin.

But if a word be spoken, Its beau - ty to con-
Doch kommt das Wort und fasst es und führt es vor das

vey, The spell at once is bro - ken, 'Twill
Aug; Wie Ne - bel - grau er - blasst es und

van - ish quite a - way, 'Twill
schwin - det wie ein Hauch, und

PRESS THY CHEEK AGAINST MINE OWN

(LEHN' DEINE WANG' AN MEINE WANG')

(Composed in 1856)

(Original Key)

HEINRICH HEINE (1799 - 1856)
Translated by Louis C. Elson

ADOLF JENSEN, Op.1, No 1
(1837-1889)

Oh, press thy cheek a-gainst mine own; To-
Lehn' dei - ne Wang an mei - ne Wang,

geth - er our tears shall be flow - ing,
flie - ssen die Thrä - nen zu - sam - men,

And press thy heart   close to my heart,   To - geth - er the
und   an   mein Herz   drück' fest dein Herz,   dann schla - gen zu-

flames__ shall be   glow - ing;   And   when   in   the
sam - men die   Flam - men.   Und   wenn   in   die

glow - ing   flames   at   last,   The   streams   of   tears   are
gro - sse   Flam - me   fliesst   der   Strom   von   un - sern

throng - ing,
Thrä - nen,
And, when my arm shall en - cir - cle thee
und wenn mein Arm dich ge - wal - tig um -

fast,
schliesst,
Then I shall die of long - - ing;
sterb' ich vor Lie - bes - seh - - nen.

Oh, press thy cheek a - gainst mine own! _____
Lehn' dei - ne Wang' an mei - ne Wang! _____

WHEN THROUGH THE PIAZZETTA
(WENN DURCH DIE PIAZZETTA)

(Composed in 1874)

(Original Key)

THOMAS MOORE (1779-1852)
German translation by Ferd. Freiligrath

ADOLF JENSEN, Op.50, No 3
(1837-1889)

ROW GENTLY HERE, MY GONDOLIER!
(LEIS' RUDERN HIER, MEIN GONDOLIER!)

(Composed in 1874)

(Original Key)

THOMAS MOORE (1779-1852)
German translation by Ferd. Freiligrath

ADOLF JENSEN, Op.50, No. 4
(1837-1889)

133

WHY?
(WARUM?)

(Composed in 1869)

(Original Key)

+)HEINRICH HEINE (1799-1856)
Translated by Natalia Macfarren

PIOTR ILYITCH TCHAÏKOVSKY
Op. 6, N° 5
(1840-1893)

+) **The retention of Heine's original text is not possible as the composer used a Russian translation in a different metre.**

NONE BUT THE LONELY HEART
(NUR WER DIE SEHNSUCHT KENNT)

(Composed in 1869)

(Original Key, D♭)

JOHANN WOLFGANG von GOETHE (1749-1832)
Translated by Arthur Westbrook

PIOTR ILYITCH TCHAÏKOVSKY, Op.6, Nº 6
(1840-1893)

None but the lone - ly heart
Nur wer die Sehn - sucht kennt,

Can know my sad - ness; A - lone, and
weiss, was ich lei - de! Al - lein und

part - ed far From joy and glad - ness.
ab - ge - trennt von al - ler Freu - de.

Heav'n's bound - less
Seh' ich aus

un poco marcato

arch I see Spread out a - bove me. Ah! what a
Fir - ma - ment nach je - ner Sei - te. Ach! der mich

dis - tance drear To one who loves me!
liebt und kennt ist in der Wei - te.

From joy and glad - ness. My sen - ses
von al - ler Freu - de! *Es schwin-delt*

fail, A burn - ing fire de -
mir, *es brennt mein Ein - ge -*

vours me. None but the lone - ly heart Can
wei - de, *Nur wer die Sehn - sucht kennt, weiss,*

know my sad - ness.
was ich lei - de!

DISAPPOINTMENT
(DÉCEPTION)
(Composed in 1888)

(Original Key, E minor)

PAUL COLLIN
Translated by Alexander Blaess

PIOTR ILYITCH TCHAÏKOVSKY, Op. 65, Nº 2
(1840-1893)

While the sun shines in wont-ed splen-dor, The deep woods I fain would be-hold, Where__ in bliss our love we first told 'Mid sweet pledg-es and dal-lying can-dor. Thought I with

Le so-leil ra-yon-nait en-to-re J'ai vou-lu re-voir les grands bois, où____ nous pro-me-nions au-tre-fois notre a-mour a sa belle au-ro-re. Je me di-

cheer; "My love I'll meet be - low the nod-ding beech-tree yon - der,
sais: "Sur le che - min, je la re-trou-ve - rai sans dou - te,

A - gain rove through thick-ets dis - creet, Our hands en-twin'd in
ma main se ten - dra vers sa main et nous nous re - met -

si - lent won - der." Yet I seek thee, my love, in vain! I
trons en rou - te." Je re-gar-de par - tout, En vain! J'ap -

call thee! but si - lence mocks__ my plead-ing. Dark-ness fall-ing o'er
pel - le! Et l'é - cho seul__ m'é - cou - te! O, le pau-vre so -

Più mosso

Tempo I

AS MY DEAR OLD MOTHER
(ALS DIE ALTE MUTTER)
from the Gipsy Melodies

ADOLF HEYDUK (1835 –)
Translated by *Isabella G. Parker*

(Original Key)

ANTONIN DVORÁK, Op.55, No 4
(1841 – 1904)

As my — dear, old — moth — er
Als die — al - te — Mut - ter

Taught her — chil - dren, — sing - ing, Songs that from — her —
mich noch lehr - te — sin - gen, Thrä - nen in — den —

eye - lids Tears so oft were bring - ing:
Wim - pern gar so oft ihr hin - gen.

So, when for my_ chil - - dren Those old_ songs re-call__ -ing, Oft - en flow_ the_ tear - -drops, oft they flow_____ On my brown cheeks fall - ing.

Jetzt, wo ich die_ Klei - - nen sel - ber üb' im_ San - - ge, in_ den_ Bart oft, rie - selt's oft_____ von der brau - nen_ Wan - ge.

(mir vom_ Au - ge, rie - selt's oft mir auf die brau - ne_ Wan - ge.)

☆ Alternative text

ELEGY
(ÉLÉGIE)

LOUIS GALLET (1835-)
Translated by Isabella G. Parker

JULES MASSENET
(1842-)

FROM MONTE PINCIO
(VOM MONTE PINCIO)

NOCTURNE

Composed in 1870)

(Original Key)

BJÖRNSTJERNE BJÖRNSON (1832–)
Translated by F. Corder

EDVARD GRIEG
(1843 –1907)

Rapt and se - rene as the face of the dead.
klärt sich der Berg wie ein Ant - litz im Tod.

Domes in the sweet-scent-ed dis - tance are gleam-ing, Mists blue and grey o'er the
Kup - peln in duf - ti - ger Fer - ne er - glü - hen, blau-schwar-ze Ne - bel die

mead - ows come stream - ing, Roll - ing a - down as ob
Fel - der um - zie - hen, wal - len ein - her wie Ver -

li - vion has roll'd, Weav-ing a gar-ment a thousand years old.
ges - sen-heit wallt, we - ben ein Kleid, das Jahr - tau-sen - de alt.

Andante

Deep-ens the still-ness, dark-ens the day,
Stil - ler nun wird es, es dun-kelt das Blau,

And, from the ghosts of the past thus be-hold-ing,
und aus der däm-mern-den Vor - zeit Ge-stal - ten

Heav-en is sure - ly the
sieht sich der Him - mel die

fu - ture un-fold-ing, Shim-mer-ing vague-ly in gath-er-ing gray.
Zu-kunft ent-fal - ten, un - si-cher schimmernd in brü-ten-dem Grau.

Wed - ding strain, sound a - main!   Flute so gay, zith - er play!
Tö - ne denn   Hoch - zeit - sang.   Zi - ther - spiel, Flö - ten - klang!

Wed - ding strain, sound a - main!   Flute so gay,
Tö - ne denn   Hoch - zeit - sang.   Zi - ther - spiel,

zith - er play!
Flö - ten - klang!

THE FIRST PRIMROSE
(MIT EINER PRIMULA VERIS)
(Composed in 1876)

J. PAULSEN (1851 -)
Translated by F. Corder

(*Original Key*)

EDVARD GRIEG
(1843-1907)

Allegretto dolcissimo

O take, thou love-ly child of Spring, This Spring's first ten-der
Mag dir, du zar-tes Früh-lings-kind, dies er-ste Blüm-chen

flow-er. De-spise it not that la-ter on Fair
from-men. Em-pfang' es gern, ver-schmäh' es nicht, weil

ros-es June will show-er. The sum-mer has its
spä-ter Ro-sen kom-men. Wohl köst-lich ist die

gold-en charm, In au-tumn hearts are gay,_____ But
Som-mer-zeit, der Herbst er-quickt das Herz,_____ der

A SWAN
(EIN SCHWAN)

(Composed in 1876)

(Original Key)

HENRIK IBSEN (1828-1906)
Translated by Frederic Field Bullard

EDVARD GRIEG
(1843-1907)

My swan, my treas - ure, With snow-y-white feath - er, Of his songs sang me nev - er A sin - gle meas - ure. Shy - ly fear - ing the elves in the bush - es, Gli - ded he, list -'ning the

Mein Schwan, mein stil - ler, mit wei-ssem Ge - fie - der, dei - ne won - ni - gen Lie - der ver - rieth kein Tril - ler. Ängst - lich sor - gend des El - fen im Grun - de, glittst du hor - chend all -

AT THE BROOKSIDE
(AN EINEM BACHE)

(Composed in 1880)

(Original Key)

A. O. VINJE (1818–1870)
Translated by Frederic Field Bullard

EDVARD GRIEG
(1843–1907)

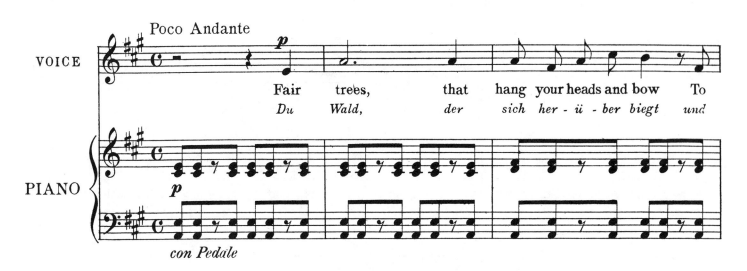

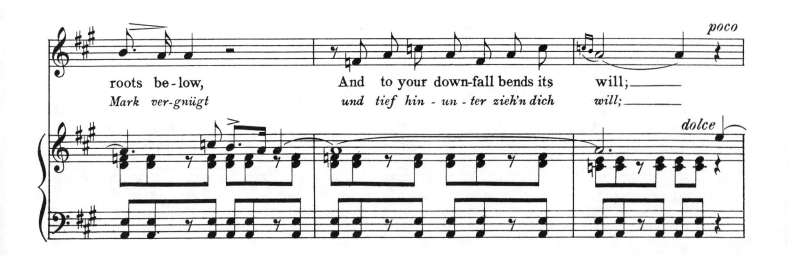

più mosso

Like you full ma - ny a one I've known, _
gleich dir hab' Man - chen ich ge - kannt _

When Life was Spring, and hope was fair, _
Im Lenz des Le - bens, frisch und roth, _

molto

Whose kiss - - es warm - ly met mine own, To
der Küs - - se drückt' auf je - ne Hand, die

THE OLD MOTHER
(DIE ALTE MUTTER)

(Composed in 1880)

(Original Key)

A. O. VINJE (1818-1870)
Translated by F. Corder

EDVARD GRIEG
(1843-1907)

THE MOUNTAIN MAID
(DAS KIND DER BERGE)

(Composed in 1898)

(Original Key, E minor)

ARNE GARBORG (1851-   )
German text by Eugen von Enzberg

EDVARD GRIEG, Op. 67, No 2
(1843-1907)

voice,— her mien,—— her look—— A strange, gloom-y calm be-
bär - de. *Mie - ne und Wort__ ver - räth die - se düst - re*

tray, gloom-y calm be-tray.__ 'Neath her
Ruh; die - se düst - re Ruh'!__ *Un - ter'm*

fore - head, beau - teous, but low, Shine her eyes with a veil - ed
dunk - eln lo - cki - gen Haar strahlt das Au - ge mit mat - tem

gleam; Some__ world that we know not she sees;__ She
Schein; sie__ starrt wie im Traum vor sich hin_____ in

FLORIAN'S SONG
(CHANSON DE FLORIAN)

(Original Key)

J.P. CLARIS de FLORIAN (1755-1794)
Translated by Laura M. Underwood

BENJAMIN GODARD
(1849-1895)

faith has he.
a ma foi.

Are echo-ing woods his songs re - peat -
Si par sa voix tendre et plain - ti -

ing, Charmed by his voice, that sweet com - plains, And do his
ve Il char - me l'é - cho de vos bois, Si les ac -

pipe's mel - o - dious strains The hearts of maid-ens set a - beat - ing, Then 'tis my
cents de son haut - bois Ren - dent la ber - gè - re pen - si - ve, C'est en - cor

love! Give him to me! I have his heart,— my faith has he.
lui, ren - dez - le moi! J'ai son a - mour,— il a ma foi.

To Ladislaus Mickiewicz

AH! THE TORMENT!
(ACH! DIE QUALEN)

(Original Key)

ADAM MICKIEWICZ (1798-1855)
Translated by Isabella G. Parker

IGNACE JAN PADEREWSKI, Op.18, Nº 5
(1859—)

How my heart with bit-ter pangs is
Ach! die Qua-len die mein Herz durch-

ra-ging!___ Death were on-ly joy, such pain as-sua-ging.___
wüh-len!___ Nur der Todt kann sie für e-wig stil-len:___

THE SEA

(Composed in 1892)

(Original Key, D)

WILLIAM DEAN HOWELLS (1887-   )

EDWARD A. MacDOWELL, Op.47, No7
(1861-1908)

SERENADE
(STÄNDCHEN)
(1886)

(Original Key)

ADOLF FRIEDRICH von SCHACK (1815-1894)
Translated by Isabella G. Parker

RICHARD STRAUSS, Op 17, Nº 2
(1864 –)

A - wake!_____ a - wake!_____ and soft - ly a - rise._____ None oth-er from slum - ber a-wa-ken! The

Mach' auf,_____ mach' auf,_____ doch lei - se, mein Kind,_____ um Kei-nen vom Schlum - mer zu we-cken, kaum